This book belongs to...

This book was a gift from...

Meet Stanley: The Reading Dog

By Rebecca Barker Bridges

Photographed by Laura Rogers

GOLDEN
GATE
PUBLISHING

Published by Golden Gate Publishing, San Francisco, CA USA
www.GoldenGatePublish.com
Twitter: @GoldenGatePub

Photographs by Laura Rogers
Cover Design by Ramon Abad

For information regarding permission, please write to:
Golden Gate Publishing, Attention: Permissions Department
P.O. Box 27478, San Francisco, CA 94127 U.S.A.
Or GoldenGatePublishing@gmail.com

Golden Gate Publishing authors are available for select speaking events.
To contact us please email GoldenGatePublishing@gmail.com.

This book was printed in the United States of America.

ISBN 978-0-9856631-6-2
Library of Congress Control Number: 2014948919

Dedication

This book is dedicated to Stanley and all the countless hours he has spent bringing joy and warmth to those around him. Also, a special thanks goes out to Laura Rogers for her fantastic job capturing Stanley "in action" and to all of my wonderful students who helped make this book a reality. Lastly, I owe a huge thank you to my loving husband, whose encouragement and faith helped me get to the finish line!

Stanley has
a big job.

He trained for
many months
and had to work
hard to pass
tough tests.

He is not
a firefighter.

Or even a pilot.

But his
job is just as
important.

Stanley is a reading dog!

No, Stanley is not a doggy genius...

He cannot read the words out loud.

But, he is an
EXPERT listener.

He is trained
to listen to
children read.

And listen he does!
Day after day...

It's his
favorite activity!

Every morning,
Stanley wakes
up, brushes his
teeth, and goes
to work!

He gets to meet lots of children.

They pet him and scratch behind his ears.

Then they grab
a book to read
and sit in a
beanbag chair.

That's when
Stanley knows
it's time for work!

He lies down next to the beanbag chair and gets ready to listen.

Some stories are scary and Stanley gets fearful.

Some stories are
happy and
Stanley smiles.

Some stories are
very long and
Stanley gets sleepy.

But most importantly, Stanley ALWAYS listens.

He is very
encouraging,
supportive,
and patient.

Stanley doesn't care if a child reads fast or slow.

He likes it
just the same and
never judges
or criticizes.

He makes the children feel comfortable
and confident when they read.

As long as Stanley gets to hear a good story
and gets some pats on the head...

he is a
happy
camper.

Now that's a good job!

Write Your Own Letter to Stanley!

Please mail your letter to:

Stanley, The Reading Dog
P.O. Box 460814
San Francisco, CA 94146-0814

or email letter to:
StanleyTheReadingDog@gmail.com

Dear Stanley,

Yours truly,

Draw a Picture of
You and Stanley!

My Favorite Books I Would Read to Stanley
(or a Dog Like Stanley)

_____

_____

_____

_____

_____

Follow Stanley:

Twitter: @ReadToStanley

Instagram: @ReadToStanley

Facebook: Stanley The Reading Dog

Coming in 2015

Meet Stanley: The Big Brother

Look for it in a bookstore near you!

About the Author

Rebecca Barker Bridges graduated from Brown University with a B.A. in Education, then earned her M.Ed. in Educational Therapy at Holy Names University. She worked for 8 years in Bay Area Independent Schools as a teacher and Learning Specialist before opening Bridges to Learning, her Educational Therapy private practice. At Bridges to Learning, Rebecca, along with her dog and business partner, Stanley, focus on reading remediation for students with learning difficulties. Stanley, a certified therapy dog, is integral to Rebecca's practice. She has had the benefit of seeing first hand the profound effect that reading to a therapy dog has on a child's confidence and reading fluency. In addition to her work as an Educational Therapist, Rebecca volunteers with the SPCA Puppy Dog Tales Program and visits local libraries with Stanley. She lives in San Francisco with her Golden Retriever, Stanley, and the rest of her loving family.